SOME POEMS OF CHILDHOOD

SOME POEMS OF CHILDHOOD

By EUGENE FIELD

Selected by BERTHA E. MAHONY
Illustrated by GERTRUDE A. KAY

CHARLES SCRIBNER'S SONS
NEW YORK
1937

FOREWORD

Happily in spite of our swiftly changing life today, little homes do still exist with flowers peering in the doors and children peering out. There continue to be, in spite of radios, people who like to sing, and who know how to create wild prancing steeds of knee and ankle on which small people go galloping, galloping. In these homes, there is a pleasant place for Eugene Field's lullabies, bedtime songs and verses of children at play.

Almost every poem in this collection is a home poem. The quality which makes these poems different from all other verses for childhood and which gives them so distinct a place in nursery literature is that they express the feelings of a light-hearted young father; a father who remembered with great particularity his own feelings as a small child and as a boy; a father who was interested in all the phases of children's thoughts and feelings, ways and plays. We have much verse of mother love and much verse expressive of childhood interests but no other considerable volume of verse so completely and spontaneously expressive of the father.

Some of the poems have as background the woods and fields and flowers of New England as Eugene Field knew them when he lived as a boy with the cousin who mothered him in Amherst, Massachusetts. He was born in St. Louis, Missouri, in

September, 1850, but he had New England in his blood from his Vermont father. He died in Buena Park, Illinois, November 4, 1895.

Probably his readers will never think the less of Eugene Field if they know that he cared little for school. Schools in those days were not perhaps so interesting as now. He spent short terms in three colleges—Williams, Knox and the University of Missouri—but it was when he began work on a newspaper in Chicago that he undertook his own education in earnest with a desire to make up for lost time. No one in college had thought him more than passingly interested in the Latin poets, but once out, he developed a vital interest in Horace. He strove steadily also to improve his writing ability by reading the best prose and poetry of the fifteenth and sixteenth centuries.

The times change, people change and verse forms, like all other arts, change. Let us hope that homes, while changing always toward greater sincerity and joy, remain with us, filled with the love and life of children, and with time for poetry and song.

BERTHA E. MAHONY.

July, 1931

CONTENTS

vii

CHILDREN'S PLAY

PITTYPAT AND TIPPYTOE

All day long they come and go—
Pittypat and Tippytoe;
   Footprints up and down the hall,
      Playthings scattered on the floor,
   Finger-marks along the wall,
      Tell-tale smudges on the door—
By these presents you shall know
Pittypat and Tippytoe.

How they riot at their play!
And a dozen times a day
   In they troop, demanding bread—
      Only buttered bread will do,
   And that butter must be spread
      Inches thick with sugar too!
And I never can say, "No,
Pittypat and Tippytoe!"

Sometimes there are griefs to soothe,
Sometimes ruffled brows to smooth;
    For (I much regret to say)
        Tippytoe and Pittypat
    Sometimes interrupt their play
        With an internecine spat;
Fie, for shame! to quarrel so—
Pittypat and Tippytoe!

Oh, the thousand worrying things
Every day recurrent brings!
    Hands to scrub and hair to brush,
        Search for playthings gone amiss,
    Many a wee complaint to hush,
        Many a little bump to kiss;
Life seems one vain, fleeting show
To Pittypat and Tippytoe!

And when day is at an end,
There are little duds to mend:
    Little frocks are strangely torn,
        Little shoes great holes reveal,
    Little hose, but one day worn,
        Rudely yawn at toe and heel!
Who but *you* could work such woe,
Pittypat and Tippytoe?

But when comes this thought to me:
"Some there are that childless be,"
   Stealing to their little beds,
      With a love I cannot speak,
   Tenderly I stroke their heads—
      Fondly kiss each velvet cheek.
God help those who do not know
A Pittypat or Tippytoe!

On the floor and down the hall,
Rudely smutched upon the wall,
   There are proofs in every kind
      Of the havoc they have wrought,
   And upon my heart you 'd find
      Just such trade-marks, if you sought;
Oh, how glad I am 't is so,
Pittypat and Tippytoe!

GOOD–CHILDREN STREET

There 's a dear little home in Good-Children street—
    My heart turneth fondly to-day
Where tinkle of tongues and patter of feet
    Make sweetest of music at play;
Where the sunshine of love illumines each face
And warms every heart in that old-fashioned place.

For dear little children go romping about
  With dollies and tin tops and drums,
And, my! how they frolic and scamper and shout
  Till bedtime too speedily comes!
Oh, days they are golden and days they are fleet
With little folk living in Good-Children street.

15

See, here comes an army with guns painted red,
  And swords, caps, and plumes of all sorts;
The captain rides gayly and proudly ahead
  On a stick-horse that prances and snorts!
Oh, legions of soldiers you 're certain to meet—
Nice make-believe soldiers—in Good-Children street.

And yonder Odette wheels her dolly about—
    Poor dolly! I 'm sure she is ill,
For one of her blue china eyes has dropped out
    And her voice is asthmatic'ly shrill.
Then, too, I observe she is minus her feet,
Which causes much sorrow in Good-Children street.

'T is so the dear children go romping about
 With dollies and banners and drums,
And I venture to say they are sadly put out
 When an end to their jubilee comes:
Oh, days they are golden and days they are fleet
With little folk living in Good-Children street!

But when falleth night over river and town,
 Those little folk vanish from sight,
And an angel all white from the sky cometh down
 And guardeth the babes through the night,
And singeth her lullabies tender and sweet
To the dear little people in Good-Children street.

Though elsewhere the world be o'erburdened with care,
 Though poverty fall to my lot,
Though toil and vexation be always my share,
 What care I—they trouble me not!
This thought maketh life ever joyous and sweet:
There's a dear little home in Good-Children street.

THE HAWTHORNE CHILDREN

The Hawthorne children—seven in all—
    Are famous friends of mine,
And with what pleasure I recall
How, years ago, one gloomy fall,
    I took a tedious railway line
And journeyed by slow stages down
Unto that sleepy seaport town
    (Albeit one worth seeing),
  Where Hildegarde, John, Henry, Fred,
And Beatrix and Gwendolen
And she that was the baby then—
    These famous seven, as aforesaid,
      Lived, moved, and had their being.

The Hawthorne children gave me such
    A welcome by the sea,
That the eight of us were soon in touch,
And though their mother marvelled much,
    Happy as larks were we!
Egad I was a boy again
With Henry, John, and Gwendolen!
    And, oh! the funny capers
    I cut with Hildegarde and Fred!
The pranks we heedless children played,
The deafening, awful noise we made—
    'T would shock my family, if they read
    About it in the papers!

The Hawthorne children all were smart;
    The girls, as I recall,
Had comprehended every art
Appealing to the head and heart,
    The boys were gifted, all;
'T was Hildegarde who showed me how
To hitch the horse and milk a cow
    And cook the best of suppers;
  With Beatrix upon the sands
I sprinted daily, and was beat,
While Henry stumped me to the feat
    Of walking round upon my hands
      Instead of on my "uppers."

The Hawthorne children liked me best
    Of evenings, after tea;
For then, by general request,
I spun them yarns about the west—
    And *all* involving Me!
I represented how I'd slain
The bison on the gore-smeared plain,

And divers tales of wonder
  I told of how I'd fought and bled
In Injun scrimmages galore,
Till Mrs. Hawthorne quoth, "No more!"
  And packed her darlings off to bed
  To dream of blood and thunder!

They must have changed a deal since then:
  The misses tall and fair,
And those three lusty, handsome men,
Would they be girls and boys again
  Were I to happen there,
Down in that spot beside the sea
Where we made such tumultuous glee
  In dull autumnal weather?
  Ah me! the years go swiftly by,
And yet how fondly I recall
The week when we were children all—
  Dear Hawthorne children, you and I—
  Just eight of us, together!

THE DINKEY–BIRD

In an ocean, 'way out yonder
  (As all sapient people know),
Is the land of Wonder-Wander,
  Whither children love to go;
It 's their playing, romping, swinging,
  That give great joy to me
While the Dinkey-Bird goes singing
  In the amfalula tree!

There the gum-drops grow like cherries,
    And taffy 's thick as peas—
Caramels you pick like berries
    When, and where, and how you please;
Big red sugar-plums are clinging
    To the cliffs beside that sea
Where the Dinkey-Bird is singing
    In the amfalula tree.

So when children shout and scamper
   And make merry all the day,
When there's naught to put a damper
   To the ardor of their play;
When I hear their laughter ringing,
   Then I'm sure as sure can be
That the Dinkey-Bird is singing
   In the amfalula tree.

For the Dinkey-Bird's bravuras
   And staccatos are so sweet—
His roulades, appoggiaturas,
   And robustos so complete,
That the youth of every nation—
   Be they near or far away—
Have especial delectation
   In that gladsome roundelay.

Their eyes grow bright and brighter,
   Their lungs begin to crow,
Their hearts get light and lighter,
   And their cheeks are all aglow;
For an echo cometh bringing
   The news to all and me,
That the Dinkey-Bird is singing
   In the amfalula tree.

I'm sure you like to go there
   To see your feathered friend—
And so many goodies grow there
   You would like to comprehend!
Speed, little dreams, your winging
   To that land across the sea
Where the Dinkey-Bird is singing
   In the amfalula tree!

THE DRUM

I 'm a beautiful red, red drum,
   And I train with the soldier boys;
As up the street we come,
   Wonderful is our noise!
There 's Tom, and Jim, and Phil,
   And Dick, and Nat, and Fred,
While Widow Cutler's Bill
   And I march on ahead,
With a r-r-rat-tat-tat
   And a tum-titty-um-tum-tum—
Oh, there 's bushels of fun in that
   For boys with a little red drum!

The Injuns came last night
   While the soldiers were abed,
And they gobbled a Chinese kite
   And off to the woods they fled!
The woods are the cherry-trees
   Down in the orchard lot,
And the soldiers are marching to seize
   The booty the Injuns got.
With tum-titty-um-tum-tum,
   And r-r-rat-tat-tat,
When soldiers marching come
   Injuns had better scat!

Step up there, little Fred,
   And, Charley, have a mind!
Jim is as far ahead
   As you two are behind!
Ready with gun and sword
   Your valorous work to do—
Yonder the Injun horde
   Are lying in wait for you.
And their hearts go pitapat
   When they hear the soldiers come
With a r-r-rat-tat-tat
   And a tum-titty-um-tum-tum!

Course it 's all in play!
  The skulking Injun crew
That hustled the kite away
  Are little white boys, like you!
But "honest" or "just in fun,"
  It is all the same to me;
And, when the battle is won,
  Home once again march we
With a r-r-rat-tat-tat
  And tum-titty-um-tum-tum;
And there 's glory enough in that
  For the boys with their little red drum!

TEENY–WEENY

Every evening, after tea,
Teeny-Weeny comes to me,
And, astride my willing knee,
   Plies his lash and rides away;
Though that palfrey, all too spare,
Finds his burden hard to bear,
Teeny-Weeny does n't care;
   He commands, and I obey!

First it 's trot, and gallop then;
Now it 's back to trot again;
Teeny-Weeny likes it when
   He is riding fierce and fast.
Then his dark eyes brighter grow
And his cheeks are all aglow:
"More!" he cries, and never "Whoa!"
   Till the horse breaks down at last.

Oh, the strange and lovely sights
Teeny-Weeny sees of nights,
As he makes those famous flights
   On that wondrous horse of his!
Oftentimes before he knows,
Wearylike his eyelids close,
And, still smiling, off he goes
   Where the land of By-low is.

There he sees the folk of fay
Hard at ring-a-rosie play,
And he hears those fairies say:
   "Come, let 's chase him to and fro!"
But, with a defiant shout,
Teeny puts that host to rout;
Of this tale I make no doubt,
   Every night he tells it so.

So I feel a tender pride
In my boy who dares to ride
That fierce horse of his astride,
    Off into those misty lands;
And as on my breast he lies,
Dreaming in that wondrous wise,
I caress his folded eyes,
    Pat his little dimpled hands.

On a time he went away,
Just a little while to stay,
And I 'm not ashamed to say
   I was very lonely then;
Life without him was so sad,
You can fancy I was glad
And made merry when I had
   Teeny-Weeny back again!

So of evenings, after tea,
When he toddles up to me
And goes tugging at my knee,
   You should hear his palfrey neigh!
You should see him prance and shy,
When, with an exulting cry,
Teeny-Weeny, vaulting high,
   Plies his lash and rides away!

THE DUEL

The gingham dog and the calico cat
Side by side on the table sat;
'T was half-past twelve, and (what do you think!)
Nor one nor t' other had slept a wink!
    The old Dutch clock and the Chinese plate
    Appeared to know as sure as fate
There was going to be a terrible spat.
    (I was n't there; I simply state
    What was told to me by the Chinese plate!)

The gingham dog went "bow-wow-wow!"
And the calico cat replied "mee-ow!"
The air was littered, an hour or so,
With bits of gingham and calico,
    While the old Dutch clock in the chimney-place
    Up with its hands before its face,
For it always dreaded a family row!
    (Now mind: I 'm only telling you
    What the old Dutch clock declares is true!)

The Chinese plate looked very blue,
And wailed, "Oh, dear! what shall we do!"
But the gingham dog and the calico cat
Wallowed this way and tumbled that,
    Employing every tooth and claw
    In the awfullest way you ever saw—
And, oh! how the gingham and calico flew!
    (Don't fancy I exaggerate—
    I got my news from the Chinese plate!)

Next morning, where the two had sat
They found no trace of dog or cat;
And some folks think unto this day
That burglars stole that pair away!
  But the truth about the cat and pup
  Is this: they ate each other up!
Now what do you really think of that!
  (*The old Dutch clock it told me so,*
  And that is how I came to know.)

THE RIDE TO BUMPVILLE

Play that my knee was a calico mare
    Saddled and bridled for Bumpville;
Leap to the back of this steed, if you dare,
    And gallop away to Bumpville!
I hope you 'll be sure to sit fast in your seat,
For this calico mare is prodigiously fleet,
And many adventures you 're likely to meet
    As you journey along to Bumpville.

This calico mare both gallops and trots
    While whisking you off to Bumpville;
She paces, she shies, and she stumbles, in spots,
    In the tortuous road to Bumpville;
And sometimes this strangely mercurial steed
Will suddenly stop and refuse to proceed,
Which, all will admit, is vexatious indeed,
    When one is en route to Bumpville!

She 's scared of the cars when the engine goes "Toot!"
    Down by the crossing at Bumpville;
You 'd better look out for that treacherous brute
    Bearing you off to Bumpville!
With a snort she rears up on her hindermost heels,
And executes jigs and Virginia reels—
Words fail to explain how embarrassed one feels
    Dancing so wildly to Bumpville!

It 's bumpytybump and it 's jiggytyjog,
   Journeying on to Bumpville;
It 's over the hilltop and down through the bog
   You ride on your way to Bumpville;
It 's rattletybang over boulder and stump,
There are rivers to ford, there are fences to jump,
And the corduroy road it goes bumpytybump,
   Mile after mile to Bumpville!

Perhaps you 'll observe it 's no easy thing
    Making the journey to Bumpville,
So I think, on the whole, it were prudent to bring
    An end to this ride to Bumpville;
For, though she has uttered no protest or plaint,
The calico mare must be blowing and faint—
What 's more to the point, I 'm blowed if I ain't!
    So play we have got to Bumpville!

"BOOH!"

On afternoons, when baby boy has had a splendid nap,
And sits, like any monarch on his throne, in nurse's lap,
In some such wise my handkerchief I hold before my face,
And cautiously and quietly I move about the place;
Then, with a cry, I suddenly expose my face to view,
And you should hear him laugh and crow when I say "Booh!"

44

Sometimes the rascal tries to make believe that he is scared,
And really, when I first began, he stared, and stared, and
    stared;
And then his under lip came out and farther out it came,
Till mamma and the nurse agreed it was a "cruel shame"—
But now what does that same wee, toddling, lisping baby do
But laugh and kick his little heels when I say "Booh!"

He laughs and kicks his little heels in rapturous glee, and then
In shrill, despotic treble bids me "do it all aden!"
And I—of course I do it; for, as his progenitor,
It is such pretty, pleasant play as this that I am for!
And it is, oh, such fun! and I am sure that we shall rue
The time when we are both too old to play the game of "Booh!"

LITTLE BOY BLUE

The little toy dog is covered with dust,
　　But sturdy and stanch he stands;
And the little toy soldier is red with rust,
　　And his musket moulds in his hands.
Time was when the little toy dog was new,
　　And the soldier was passing fair;
And that was the time when our Little Boy Blue
　　Kissed them and put them there.

"Now, don't you go till I come," he said,
　　"And don't you make any noise!"
So, toddling off to his trundle-bed,
　　He dreamt of the pretty toys;
And, as he was dreaming, an angel song
　　Awakened our Little Boy Blue—
Oh! the years are many, the years are long,
　　But the little toy friends are true!

Aye, faithful to Little Boy Blue they stand,
　　Each in the same old place—
Awaiting the touch of a little hand,
　　The smile of a little face;
And they wonder, as waiting the long years through
　　In the dust of that little chair,
What has become of our Little Boy Blue,
　　Since he kissed them and put them there.

JEST 'FORE CHRISTMAS

Father calls me William, sister calls me Will,
Mother calls me Willie, but the fellers call me Bill!
Mighty glad I ain't a girl—ruther be a boy,
Without them sashes, curls, an' things that's worn by Fauntleroy!
Love to chawnk green apples an' go swimmin' in the lake—
Hate to take the castor-ile they give for belly-ache!
'Most all the time, the whole year round, there ain't no flies
    on me,
But jest 'fore Christmas I'm as good as I kin be!

Got a yeller dog named Sport, sick him on the cat;
First thing she knows she does n't know where she is at!
Got a clipper sled, an' when us kids goes out to slide,
'Long comes the grocery cart, an' we all hook a ride!
But sometimes when the grocery man is worrited an' cross,
He reaches at us with his whip, an' larrups up his hoss,
An' then I laff an' holler, "Oh, ye never teched *me!*"
But jest 'fore Christmas I'm as good as I kin be!

Gran'ma says she hopes that when I git to be a man,
I'll be a missionarer like her oldest brother, Dan,
As was et up by the cannibuls that lives in Ceylon's Isle,
Where every prospeck pleases, an' only man is vile!

But gran'ma she has never been to see a Wild West show,
Nor read the Life of Daniel Boone, or else I guess she'd know
That Buff'lo Bill an' cow-boys is good enough for me!
Excep' jest 'fore Christmas, when I 'm good as I kin be!

And then old Sport he hangs around, so solemn-like an' still,
His eyes they seem a-sayin': "What 's the matter, little Bill?"
The old cat sneaks down off her perch an' wonders what 's be-
    come
Of them two enemies of hern that used to make things hum!
But I am so perlite an' 'tend so earnestly to biz,
That mother says to father: "How improved our Willie is!"
But father, havin' been a boy hisself, suspicions me
When, jest 'fore Christmas, I 'm as good as I kin be!

For Christmas, with its lots an' lots of candies, cakes, an' toys,
Was made, they say, for proper kids, an' not for naughty boys;
So wash yer face an' bresh yer hair, an' mind yer p's and q's,
An' don't bust out yer pantaloons, and don't wear out yer shoes;
Say "Yessum" to the ladies, an' "Yessur" to the men,
An' when they 's company, don't pass yer plate for pie again;
But, thinkin' of the things yer 'd like to see upon that tree,
Jest 'fore Christmas be as good as yer kin be!

WITH TRUMPET AND DRUM

With big tin trumpet and little red drum,
Marching like soldiers, the children come!
    It 's this way and that way they circle and file—
        My! but that music of theirs is fine!
    This way and that way, and after a while
        They march straight into this heart of mine!
A sturdy old heart, but it has to succumb
To the blare of that trumpet and beat of that drum!

Come on, little people, from cot and from hall—
This heart it hath welcome and room for you all!
    It will sing you its songs and warm you with love,
        As your dear little arms with my arms intertwine;

It will rock you away to the dreamland above—
    Oh, a jolly old heart is this old heart of mine,
And jollier still is it bound to become
When you blow that big trumpet and beat that red drum!

So come; though I see not *his* dear little face
And hear not *his* voice in this jubilant place,
    I know he were happy to bid me enshrine
        His memory deep in my heart with your play—
    Ah me! but a love that *is* sweeter than mine
        Holdeth my boy in its keeping to-day!
And my heart it is lonely—so, little folk, come,
March in and make merry with trumpet and drum!

LITTLE MISS BRAG

Little Miss Brag has much to say
To the rich little lady from over the way,
And the rich little lady puts out a lip
As she looks at her own white, dainty slip,
And wishes that *she* could wear a gown
As pretty as gingham of faded brown!
For little Miss Brag she lays much stress
On the privileges of a gingham dress—
   "Aha,
   Oho!"

The rich little lady from over the way
Has beautiful dolls in vast array;
Yet she envies the raggedy home-made doll
She hears our little Miss Brag extol.
For the raggedy doll can fear no hurt
From wet, or heat, or tumble, or dirt!
Her nose is inked, and her mouth is, too,
And one eye 's black and the other 's blue—
   "Aha,
    Oho!"

55

The rich little lady goes out to ride
With footmen standing up outside,
Yet wishes that, sometimes, after dark
Her father would trundle *her* in the park;—
That, sometimes, *her* mother would sing the things
Little Miss Brag says *her* mother sings
When through the attic window streams
The moonlight full of golden dreams—
                    "Aha,
                      Oho!"

Yes, little Miss Brag has much to say
To the rich little lady from over the way;
And yet who knows but from her heart
Often the bitter sighs upstart—
Uprise to lose their burn and sting
In the grace of the tongue that loves to sing
Praise of the treasures all its own!
So I've come to love that treble tone—
                    "Aha,
                      Oho!"

BEDTIME SONGS AND LULLABIES

THE SONG OF LUDDY–DUD

A sunbeam comes a-creeping
   Into my dear one's nest,
And sings to our babe a-sleeping,
    ' The song that I love the best:
        " 'T is little Luddy-Dud in the morning—
      'T is little Luddy-Dud at night;
        And all day long
        'T is the same sweet song
Of that waddling, toddling, coddling little mite,
    Luddy-Dud."

The bird to the tossing clover,
  The bee to the swaying bud,
Keep singing that sweet song over
  Of wee little Luddy-Dud.
        " 'T is little Luddy-Dud in the morning—
      'T is little Luddy-Dud at night;
          And all day long
            'T is the same dear song
Of that growing, crowing, knowing little sprite,
    Luddy-Dud!"

Luddy-Dud's cradle is swinging
  Where softly the night winds blow,
And Luddy-Dud's mother is singing
  A song that is sweet and low:
        " 'T is little Luddy-Dud in the morning—
      'T is little Luddy-Dud at night;
          And all day long
            'T is the same sweet song
Of my nearest and my dearest heart's delight,
    Luddy-Dud!"

FAIRY AND CHILD

Oh, listen, little Dear-My-Soul,
　To the fairy voices calling,
For the moon is high in the misty sky
　And the honey dew is falling;
To the midnight feast in the clover bloom
　The bluebells are a-ringing,
And it 's "Come away to the land of fay"
　That the katydid is singing.

Oh, slumber, little Dear-My-Soul,
　And hand in hand we 'll wander—
Hand in hand to the beautiful land
　Of Balow, away off yonder;
Or we 'll sail along in a lily leaf
　Into the white moon's halo—
Over a stream of mist and dream
　Into the land of Balow.

Or, you shall have two beautiful wings—
  Two gossamer wings and airy,
And all the while shall the old moon smile
  And think you a little fairy;
And you shall dance in the velvet sky,
  And the silvery stars shall twinkle
And dream sweet dreams as over their beams
  Your footfalls softly tinkle.

HUSHABY, SWEET MY OWN

Fair is the castle up on the hill—
    Hushaby, sweet my own!
The night is fair, and the waves are still,
And the wind is singing to you and to me
In this lowly home beside the sea—
    Hushaby, sweet my own!

On yonder hill is store of wealth—
    Hushaby, sweet my own!
And revellers drink to a little one's health;
But you and I bide night and day
For the other love that has sailed away—
    Hushaby, sweet my own!

See not, dear eyes, the forms that creep
    Ghostlike, O my own!
Out of the mists of the murmuring deep;
Oh, see them not and make no cry
Till the angels of death have passed us by—
    Hushaby, sweet my own!

Ah, little they reck of you and me—
    Hushaby, sweet my own!
In our lonely home beside the sea;
They seek the castle up on the hill,
And there they will do their ghostly will—
    Hushaby, O my own!

Here by the sea a mother croons
    "Hushaby, sweet my own!"
In yonder castle a mother swoons
While the angels go down to the misty deep
Bearing a little one fast asleep—
    Hushaby, sweet my own!

NORSE LULLABY

The sky is dark and the hills are white
As the storm-king speeds from the north to-night;
And this is the song the storm-king sings,
As over the world his cloak he flings:
    "Sleep, sleep, little one, sleep";
He rustles his wings and gruffly sings:
    "Sleep, little one, sleep."

On yonder mountain-side a vine
Clings at the foot of a mother pine;
The tree bends over the trembling thing,
And only the vine can hear her sing:
    "Sleep, sleep, little one, sleep—
What shall you fear when I am here?
    Sleep, little one, sleep."

The king may sing in his bitter flight,
The tree may croon to the vine to-night,
But the little snowflake at my breast
Liketh the song *I* sing the best—
    Sleep, sleep, little one, sleep;
Weary thou art, a-next my heart
    Sleep, little one, sleep.

LITTLE BLUE PIGEON

Sleep, little pigeon, and fold your wings—
  Little blue pigeon with velvet eyes;
Sleep to the singing of mother-bird swinging—
  Swinging the nest where her little one lies.

Away out yonder I see a star—
   Silvery star with a tinkling song;
To the soft dew falling I hear it calling—
   Calling and tinkling the night along.

In through the window a moonbeam comes—
   Little gold moonbeam with misty wings;
All silently creeping, it asks: "Is he sleeping—
   Sleeping and dreaming while mother sings?"

Up from the sea there floats the sob
   Of the waves that are breaking upon the shore,
As though they were groaning in anguish, and moaning—
   Bemoaning the ship that shall come no more.

But sleep, little pigeon, and fold your wings—
Little blue pigeon with mournful eyes;
Am I not singing?—see, I am swinging—
Swinging the nest where my darling lies.

THE ROCK–A–BY LADY

The Rock-a-By Lady from Hushaby street
    Comes stealing; comes creeping;
The poppies they hang from her head to her feet,
And each hath a dream that is tiny and fleet—
She bringeth her poppies to you, my sweet,
    When she findeth you sleeping!

There is one little dream of a beautiful drum—
"Rub-a-dub!" it goeth;
There is one little dream of a big sugar-plum,
And lo! thick and fast the other dreams come
Of popguns that bang, and tin tops that hum,
And a trumpet that bloweth!

And dollies peep out of those wee little dreams
    With laughter and singing;
And boats go a-floating on silvery streams,
And the stars peek-a-boo with their own misty gleams,
And up, up, and up, where the Mother Moon beams,
    The fairies go winging!

Would you dream all these dreams that are tiny and fleet?
    They 'll come to you sleeping;
So shut the two eyes that are weary, my sweet,
For the Rock-a-By Lady from Hushaby street,
With poppies that hang from her head to her feet,
    Comes stealing; comes creeping.

WYNKEN, BLYNKEN, AND NOD

Wynken, Blynken, and Nod one night
   Sailed off in a wooden shoe—
Sailed on a river of crystal light,
   Into a sea of dew.
"Where are you going, and what do you wish?"
   The old moon asked the three.
"We have come to fish for the herring fish
   That live in this beautiful sea;
   Nets of silver and gold have we!"
       Said Wynken,
       Blynken,
       And Nod.

The old moon laughed and sang a song,
    As they rocked in the wooden shoe,
And the wind that sped them all night long
    Ruffled the waves of dew.
The little stars were the herring fish
    That lived in that beautiful sea—
"Now cast your nets wherever you wish—
    Never afeard are we";
So cried the stars to the fishermen three:
      Wynken,
      Blynken,
      And Nod.

All night long their nets they threw
   To the stars in the twinkling foam—
Then down from the skies came the wooden shoe,
   Bringing the fishermen home;
'T was all so pretty a sail it seemed
   As if it could not be,
And some folks thought 't was a dream they 'd dreamed
   Of sailing that beautiful sea—
   But I shall name you the fishermen three:
         Wynken,
         Blynken,
         And Nod.

Wynken and Blynken are two little eyes,
    And Nod is a little head,
And the wooden shoe that sailed the skies
    Is a wee one's trundle-bed.
So shut your eyes while mother sings
    Of wonderful sights that be,
And you shall see the beautiful things
    As you rock in the misty sea,
    Where the old shoe rocked the fishermen three:
            Wynken,
            Blynken,
            And Nod.

81

LADY BUTTON–EYES

When the busy day is done,
And my weary little one
Rocketh gently to and fro;
When the night winds softly blow,
And the crickets in the glen
Chirp and chirp and chirp again;
When upon the haunted green
Fairies dance around their queen—
Then from yonder misty skies
Cometh Lady Button-Eyes.

Through the murk and mist and gloam,
To our quiet, cosey home,
Where to singing, sweet and low,
Rocks a cradle to and fro;
Where the clock's dull monotone
Telleth of the day that 's done;
Where the moonbeams hover o'er
Playthings sleeping on the floor—
Where my weary wee one lies
Cometh Lady Button-Eyes.

Cometh like a fleeting ghost
From some distant eerie coast;
Never footfall can you hear
As that spirit fareth near—
Never whisper, never word
From that shadow-queen is heard.
In ethereal raiment dight,
From the realm of fay and sprite
In the depth of yonder skies
Cometh Lady Button-Eyes.

Layeth she her hands upon
My dear weary little one,
And those white hands overspread
Like a veil the curly head,
Seem to fondle and caress
Every little silken tress;
Then she smooths the eyelids down
Over those two eyes of brown—
In such soothing, tender wise
Cometh Lady Button-Eyes.

Dearest, feel upon your brow
That caressing magic now;
For the crickets in the glen
Chirp and chirp and chirp again,
While upon the haunted green
Fairies dance around their queen,
And the moonbeams hover o'er
Playthings sleeping on the floor—
Hush, my sweet! from yonder skies
Cometh Lady Button-Eyes!

THE SUGAR–PLUM TREE

Have you ever heard of the Sugar-Plum Tree?
   'T is a marvel of great renown!
It blooms on the shore of the Lollipop sea
   In the garden of Shut-Eye Town;
The fruit that it bears is so wondrously sweet
   (As those who have tasted it say)
That good little children have only to eat
   Of that fruit to be happy next day.

When you've got to the tree, you would have a hard time
　　To capture the fruit which I sing;
The tree is so tall that no person could climb
　　To the boughs where the sugar-plums swing!
But up in that tree sits a chocolate cat,
　　And a gingerbread dog prowls below—
And this is the way you contrive to get at
　　Those sugar-plums tempting you so:

You say but the word to that gingerbread dog
 And he barks with such terrible zest
That the chocolate cat is at once all agog,
 As her swelling proportions attest.
And the chocolate cat goes cavorting around
 From this leafy limb unto that,
And the sugar-plums tumble, of course, to the ground—
 Hurrah for that chocolate cat!

There are marshmallows, gumdrops, and peppermint
    canes,
    With stripings of scarlet or gold,
And you carry away of the treasure that rains
    As much as your apron can hold!
So come, little child, cuddle closer to me
    In your dainty white nightcap and gown,
And I 'll rock you away to that Sugar-Plum Tree
    In the garden of Shut-Eye Town.

THE FLY–AWAY HORSE

Oh, a wonderful horse is the Fly-Away Horse
  Perhaps you have seen him before;
Perhaps, while you slept, his shadow has swept
  Through the moonlight that floats on the floor.
For it's only at night, when the stars twinkle bright,
  That the Fly-Away Horse, with a neigh
And a pull at his rein and a toss of his mane,
  Is up on his heels and away!
      The Moon in the sky,
      As he gallopeth by,
  Cries: "Oh! what a marvellous sight!"
      And the Stars in dismay
      Hide their faces away
  In the lap of old Grandmother Night.

It is yonder, out yonder, the Fly-Away Horse
  Speedeth ever and ever away—
Over meadows and lanes, over mountains and plains,
  Over streamlets that sing at their play;
And over the sea like a ghost sweepeth he,
  While the ships they go sailing below,

And he speedeth so fast that the men at the mast
　　Adjudge him some portent of woe.
　　　　"What ho there!" they cry,
　　　　As he flourishes by
　　With a whisk of his beautiful tail;
　　　　And the fish in the sea
　　　　Are as scared as can be,
From the nautilus up to the whale!

And the Fly-Away Horse seeks those far-away lands
　　You little folk dream of at night—
Where candy-trees grow, and honey-brooks flow,
　　And corn-fields with popcorn are white;
And the beasts in the wood are ever so good
　　To children who visit them there—
What glory astride of a lion to ride,
　　Or to wrestle around with a bear!
　　　　The monkeys, they say:
　　　　"Come on, let us play,"
　　And they frisk in the cocoanut-trees:
　　　　While the parrots, that cling
　　　　To the peanut-vines, sing
　　Or converse with comparative ease!

Off! scamper to bed—you shall ride him to-night!
  For, as soon as you 've fallen asleep,
With a jubilant neigh he shall bear you away
  Over forest and hillside and deep!
But tell us, my dear, all you see and you hear
  In those beautiful lands over there,
Where the Fly-Away Horse wings his far-away course
  With the wee one consigned to his care.
        Then grandma will cry
        In amazement: "Oh, my!"
    And she 'll think it could never be so;
        And only we two
        Shall know it is true—
You and I, little precious! shall know!

HEIGHO, MY DEARIE

A moonbeam floateth from the skies,
    Whispering: "Heigho, my dearie;
I would spin a web before your eyes—
A beautiful web of silver light
Wherein is many a wondrous sight
Of a radiant garden leagues away,
Where the softly tinkling lilies sway
And the snow-white lambkins are at play—
    Heigho, my dearie!"

A brownie stealeth from the vine,
        Singing: "Heigho, my dearie;
And will you hear this song of mine—
A song of the land of murk and mist
Where bideth the bud the dew hath kist?
Then let the moonbeam's web of light
Be spun before thee silvery white,
And I shall sing the livelong night—
        Heigho, my dearie!"

The night wind speedeth from the sea,
    Murmuring: "Heigho, my dearie;
I bring a mariner's prayer for thee;
So let the moonbeam veil thine eyes,
And the brownie sing thee lullabies—
But I shall rock thee to and fro,
Kissing the brow *he* loveth so.
And the prayer shall guard thy bed, I trow—
    Heigho, my dearie!"

THE SHUT-EYE TRAIN

Come, my little one, with me!
There are wondrous sights to see
 As the evening shadows fall;
 In your pretty cap and gown,
   Don't detain
   The Shut-Eye train—
"Ting-a-ling!" the bell it goeth,
"Toot-toot!" the whistle bloweth,
And we hear the warning call:
"All aboard for Shut-Eye Town!"

Over hill and over plain
Soon will speed the Shut-Eye train!
   Through the blue where bloom the stars
   And the Mother Moon looks down
        We 'll away
        To land of Fay—
   Oh, the sights that we shall see there!
   Come, my little one, with me there—
'T is a goodly train of cars—
All aboard for Shut-Eye Town!

Swifter than a wild bird's flight,
Through the realms of fleecy light
  We shall speed and speed away!
  Let the Night in envy frown—
      What care we
      How wroth she be!
  To the Balow-land above us,
  To the Balow-folk who love us,
Let us hasten while we may—
All aboard for Shut-Eye Town!

Shut-Eye Town is passing fair—
Golden dreams await us there;
   We shall dream those dreams, my dear,
   Till the Mother Moon goes down—
     See unfold
     Delights untold!
   And in those mysterious places
   We shall see beloved faces
And beloved voices hear
In the grace of Shut-Eye Town.

Heavy are your eyes, my sweet,
Weary are your little feet—
 Nestle closer up to me
 In your pretty cap and gown;
   Don't detain
   The Shut-Eye train!
 "Ting-a-ling!" the bell it goeth,
 "Toot-toot!" the whistle bloweth,
Oh, the sights that we shall see!
All aboard for Shut-Eye Town!

GOLD AND LOVE FOR DEARIE

Out on the mountain over the town,
    All night long, all night long,
The trolls go up and the trolls go down,
    Bearing their packs and singing a song;
And this is the song the hill-folk croon,
As they trudge in the light of the misty moon—
This is ever their dolorous tune:
"Gold, gold! ever more gold—
    Bright red gold for dearie!"

Deep in the hill a father delves
　　All night long, all night long;
None but the peering, furtive elves
　　Sees his toil and hears his song;
Merrily ever the cavern rings
As merrily ever his pick he swings,
And merrily ever this song he sings:
"Gold, gold! ever more gold—
　　Bright red gold for dearie!"

Mother is rocking thy lowly bed
   All night long, all night long,
Happy to smooth thy curly head,
   To hold thy hand and to sing *her* song:
'T is not of the hill-folk dwarfed and old,
Nor the song of thy father, stanch and bold,
And the burthen it beareth is not of gold;
But it 's "Love, love! nothing but love—
   Mother's love for dearie!"

NIGHTFALL IN DORDRECHT

The mill goes toiling slowly around
    With steady and solemn creak,
And my little one hears in the kindly sound
    The voice of the old mill speak.
While round and round those big white wings
    Grimly and ghostlike creep,
My little one hears that the old mill sings:
    "Sleep, little tulip, sleep!"

The sails are reefed and the nets are drawn,
　　And, over his pot of beer,
The fisher, against the morrow's dawn,
　　Lustily maketh cheer;
He mocks at the winds that caper along
　　From the far-off clamorous deep—
But we—we love their lullaby song
　　Of "Sleep, little tulip, sleep!"

Old dog Fritz in slumber sound
    Groans of the stony mart—
To-morrow how proudly he 'll trot you round,
    Hitched to our new milk-cart!
And you shall help me blanket the kine
    And fold the gentle sheep
And set the herring a-soak in brine—
    But now, little tulip, sleep!

A Dream-One comes to button the eyes
　　That wearily droop and blink,
While the old mill buffets the frowning skies
　　And scolds at the stars that wink;
Over your face the misty wings
　　Of that beautiful Dream-One sweep,
And rocking your cradle she softly sings:
　　"Sleep, little tulip, sleep!"

WOOD AND FLOWERS

LITTLE–OH–DEAR

See, what a wonderful garden is here,
Planted and trimmed for my Little-Oh-Dear!
Posies so gaudy and grass of such brown—
Search ye the country and hunt ye the town
And never ye 'll meet with a garden so queer
As this one I 've made for my Little-Oh-Dear!

Marigolds white and buttercups blue,
Lilies all dabbled with honey and dew,
The cactus that trails over trellis and wall,
Roses and pansies and violets—all
Make proper obeisance and reverent cheer
When into her garden steps Little-Oh-Dear.

And up at the top of that lavender-tree
A silver-bird singeth as only can she;
For, ever and only, she singeth the song
"I love you—I love you!" the happy day long;—
Then the echo—the echo that smiteth me here!
"I love you, I love you," my Little-Oh-Dear!

The garden may wither, the silver-bird fly—
But what careth my little precious, or I?
From her pathway of flowers that in springtime upstart
She walketh the tenderer way in my heart.
And, oh, it is always the summer-time *here*
With that song of "I love you," my Little-Oh-Dear!

TO A LITTLE BROOK

You 're not so big as you were then.
   O little brook!—
I mean those hazy summers when
We boys roamed, full of awe, beside
Your noisy, foaming, tumbling tide,
And wondered if it could be true
That there were bigger brooks than you,
   O mighty brook, O peerless brook!

All up and down this reedy place
   Where lives the brook,
We angled for the furtive dace;
The redwing-blackbird did his best
To make us think he 'd build his nest
Hard by the stream, when, like as not,
He 'd hung it in a secret spot
   Far from the brook, the telltale brook!

And often, when the noontime heat
    Parboiled the brook,
We 'd draw our boots and swing our feet
Upon the waves that, in their play,
Would tag us last and scoot away;
And mother never seemed to know
What burnt our legs and chapped them so—
    But father guessed it was the brook!

And Fido—how he loved to swim
  The cooling brook,
Whenever we 'd throw sticks for him;
And how we boys *did* wish that we
Could only swim as good as he—
Why, Daniel Webster never was
Recipient of such great applause
  As Fido, battling with the brook!

But once—O most unhappy day
  For you, my brook!—
Came Cousin Sam along that way;
And, having lived a spell out West,
Where creeks are n't counted much at best,
He neither waded, swam, nor leapt,
But, with superb indifference, *stept*
  Across that brook—our mighty brook!

Why do you scamper on your way,
  You little brook,
When I come back to you to-day?
Is it because you flee the grass
That lunges at you as you pass,
As if, in playful mood, it would
Tickle the truant if it could,
  You chuckling brook—you saucy brook?

Or is it you no longer know—
  You fickle brook—
The honest friend of long ago?
The years that kept us twain apart
Have changed my face, but not my heart—
Many and sore those years, and yet
I fancied you could not forget
  That happy time, my playmate brook!

Oh, sing again in artless glee,
  My little brook,
The song you used to sing for me—
The song that 's lingered in my ears
So soothingly these many years;
My grief shall be forgotten when
I hear your tranquil voice again
  And that sweet song, dear little brook!

LONG AGO

I once knew all the birds that came
    And nested in our orchard trees,
For every flower I had a name,—
    My friends were woodchucks, toads, and bees;
I knew where thrived in yonder glen
    What plants would soothe a stone-bruised toe—
Oh, I was very learned then,
    But that was very long ago.

I knew the spot upon the hill
   Where checkerberries could be found,
I knew the rushes near the mill
   Where pickerel lay that weighed a pound!
I knew the wood—the very tree
   Where lived the poaching, saucy crow,
And all the woods and crows knew me—
   But that was very long ago.

And pining for the joys of youth,
   I tread the old familiar spot
Only to learn this solemn truth:
   I have forgotten, am forgot.
Yet here 's this youngster at my knee
   Knows all the things I used to know;
To think I once was wise as he!—
   But that was very long ago.

I know it's folly to complain
    Of whatsoe'er the fates decree,
Yet, were not wishes all in vain,
    I tell you what my wish should be:
I'd wish to be a boy again,
    Back with the friends I used to know.
For I was, oh, so happy then—
    But that was very long ago!